The Apple and the Mountain

David Kennedy

The Apple and the Mountain

Shearsman Books

First published in the United Kingdom in 2015 by
Shearsman Books
50 Westons Hill Drive
Emersons Green
BRISTOL
BS16 7DF

Shearsman Books Ltd Registered Office
30–31 St. James Place, Mangotsfield, Bristol BS16 9JB
(this address not for correspondence)

www.shearsman.com

ISBN 978-1-84861-426-0

ACKNOWLEDGEMENTS
Acknowledgements are due to the editors of the publications
where some of these poems first appeared:
*AndOtherPoems, Hinterland, Magma, Poetry Ireland, Poetry Wales,
Shearsman, Tears in the Fence, Under the Radar* and *The Warwick Review.*

'The Rage' was first published in *Mistral* (Rack Press, 2010).
'Hortense Breastfeeding Paul' was first published in
The Emma Press Anthology of Motherhood.

Anyone working on Cézanne owes a debt to more than a hundred
years of scholarship. I have found the following bloggers and writers
particularly useful:
Nina Athanassoglou-Kallymer, Roger Fry, Susan Sidlauskas,
Tomoki Akimaru, Kurt Badt, Henri Lallemand, Griselda Pollock,
Elisabeth Reissner, Erle Loran, Theodore Reff, Richard Shiff,
Nataša Dolenc, Joni Spigler, John House, Brian Kame,
Phan Lâm Tùng, John Shannon Hendrix,
Christopher W. Tyler and Amy Ione.

Contents

To Christine, with love

The Apple

— I will astonish Paris
with a single apple!

I will recompose the city
parish by parish, arrondissements

one by one becoming effects of
Calville Blanc d'Hiver,

Reine des Reinettes,
of Provence's crisp green odours.

The fruit's bright red, opaque
yellow thoughts will turn

the sour smack of soot and zest of iron
to dew at day break.

Eiffel's rivets will bleed
with memories of geologic saps.

Paris, you are empty
but for a single apple,

painted as if God had painted it,
from all angles, all apple colours at once,

and long queues of citizens
turning slowly round and round it

in astonishment, moving
on the thoughts of its perfume.

Jas de Bouffan

'Where the winds live'
in Provençal,
two or three times
painted tilted,

taken aback,
just background for
the chestnut trees
accumulating

in him deeply
year after year
and he in them.
Trees happening

and happening
as stubborn poles,
supple structures,
light breaking through

or broken up.
Systems for knowing,
feeling, breaking
through or not, not,

in him deeply.
Veins in the eye
and in the leaf
'where the winds live'.

Still Life with Bread and Eggs (1865)

Deep in black space
    objects floating,
        primary objects,
    things of our first world

and the first world of painting:
    two onions, two eggs,
        the wine glass still found
    in cafés today, a hearty loaf,

pain de campagne
    or rough-cast baguette
        on a bunched white cloth,
    set foam, sculpted tripes,

domestic fleece, and
    a black knife
        at an angle,
    a simple tool with which

we make the world
    and a jug.
        Animal, vegetable,
    mineral. The same objects,

the world distinguished
    into groups, appear
        and appear in paintings
    two, ten, thirty years later,

an emotional vocabulary,
    a continuing conversation,
        dialogue of forms
    and planes, things

of our first world, floating free,
    being reconfigured
        deep in black space
    or sunlit space.

Portrait of Louis-Auguste Cézanne, Reading L'Evènement (1866)

Papa in his armchair throne
in his cap
palette knife patois
living room
at the Jas de Bouffan
rough impasto evidence
of work, of a person at work
reading republican news
in France profonde
far from Paris polish
Salon finish
manière couillarde
from the balls from the guts
like the thickly buttered
smears and daubs
of Paul's Sugar Pot,
Pears and Blue Cup
behind Papa's head
as he reads L'Evènement
itself a blank
as if the future's not set
the knife's dirty lesson
not done

Scipio the Negro (1867)

The brush keeps asking
'how is a body?'
The arm loosely braced
against the stool

runs with so much light
it might be bronze.
The back hums differently,
idling motor; light strokes,

dark strokes, are a rhythm
ticking over; quick shifts
in intonation. The head,
asleep, the claw-like arm

it rests on, both in shadow,
are true to light withheld,
an answer the brush
may not want but has to take.

The Bridge at Maincy (1869)

The paint runs cold.
  The bridge straddles
stiff waters. Everything joins
    forces with brown or green,

the brush strokes not accents
  or inflections,
diacritics of light,
  but stacked or propped

like broken tiles
  on collapsed shelves,
weight become structure.
  The bridge straddling

stiff water, the frozen trees,
are geometry filled in,
clotted with colour
somehow weathered

as if a moment
  built of light, of built light,
had suffered time.
  The paint runs cold.

The two trunks, entwined
front left, are the struggle
to find form, picked up
  in girders of branch

and trunk, the rickety,
    warped wood straddling
stiff water, the dissimilar arches
    of speckled stone.

The paint runs cold.
The strokes press in.
A drama of planes
    and angles and curves.

An old bridge, doing its work.
No-one would linger here
even if the strokes left room.
The paint runs cold.

Black Marble Clock (c.1870)

The traditional lemon's
a joke: this isn't still life

but a big, ballsy, 'so what'
collection of wrongness.

Black marble clock with no hands,
the stiff white cloth that rises

under its own starch, scored,
grooved, in repeating panels,

cunty conch, jug that's either
glass or metal (who cares?),

man-size cup and saucer –
bloke's salon, man cave comforts

of the mineral, opposite
of a flower arrangement.

Now imagine who would have
this picture in his wallet.

Hortense Breastfeeding Paul (1872)

Hortense dozing,
dreaming, the contents
of her content
  hidden from us,
dreaming, dozing
in a long tradition,
Isis nursing Horus,
  Memling's nursing Mary,
Corot's breastfeeding mother,
but the painting,

like Hortense,
  is turned away from
this knowledge,
  neither sacred nor sexy.
Hortense's closed eyes
do not return a gaze,
so do not confirm
  anything we think we know
about mothers, breasts or babies.
  Soft curves

of pillow and bedding
  are breast-like, body-like,
echoing Hortense.
  And the paint is quiet,
a sleepy 'nothing to see here' hum
  done quickly.
The viewer is not required.
Everyone knows what they know
and need to know: Hortense
  is breastfeeding Paul.

The Poplars (1879-80)

Poplar poles
and clotted mass
of other trees
analyse each other
outside the grounds
of the Chateau de Marcouville.

Masts, beams, shafts,
right to left, lose
definition
or, left to right,
gain stickness, stiltness
close to Pontoise.

Slanted strokes,
shabby olive,
dull, murky moss,
sluggish sage, building up
around the poles
on the banks of the Viosne.

Planted trees
organise landscape,
subdue nature
to order, to growth
of lump and pole.
Each stroke is a fragment of time.

Plate with Fruit and Pot of Preserves (1880-81)

Chardin's piled strawberries:
Titania's table-lamp!

Dark plums and green pears,
a Septemberish 'what there is'

on everyman's white plate,
dress no set. They are just there,

enough, just days where enough
or not enough happens, happens,

and even 'not enough' takes
too much time to see what's here

as 'just enough'. So speak dark plums
green pears, dull lights on a white plate.

Cézanne at Les Trois Sautets

The vault
    of large trees
        over the water.
    The vault

of large trees
    deep in the water.
        What we see
    is what we see

decomposing
    into what we see,
        like naked flesh
    entering water

in the open air
    or pre-dawn clouds
        evaporating
    as the sun hits

our eyeballs
    and our humming brain
        is skewered
    and sliced

by birdsong.
    The day rolls out
        and long before
    noon yawns,

song and brain
    blunt each other
        and nothing remains
    but a paradox:

'the manifold picture
    of nature', still
        there, and there,
    and there, the breathless,

smarting challenges
    of its suffering
        and pleasure.
    On the banks

of the Arc, he wrote,
    'I could occupy
        myself for months
    without changing place'.

The vault
    of large trees
        over the water,
    ringing with reds

and yellows,
    over the water,
        waiting to be set off
    by a touch of blue.

Les Trois Sautets: a small bridge across the River Arc near Palette where Cézanne used to paint during the last months of his life.

The Bridge at Trois Sautets

The bridge is its dark underside,
    a beautifully turned, thrown curve
        that goes with the trunk (right)
    and takes us in and out,
goes from the trunk to distort
    usual reading and form
        a weird character
  or primitive crane.

And it is an arch, a staging,
    where the noisy drama of electrons'
        after-images plays out,
  scribbles and smudges the air,
light's graffiti, light and dark splashes,
    dark bruises, building up
        shifting moments, shifting fusions,
    shifting atmospheres
of the trees beyond the bridge
        in a long, long exposure.

        The eye stares out light
      and light goes crazy
and oil's too slow – only the militant
        pencil and nervy watercolour
            keep up, keep up
      with intention and distraction
chasing each other's tails, fusing,
        the pencil forced into abstract modelling
            over the planes of splashed colour;
        keep up, keep up with
event bursting into gesture,
        gesture into event.

Houses in Provence, The Riaux Valley near L'Estaque (1883)

Here are houses
    with no key,
        each stroke the source
    of all the others,
mustard blocks,
    blue rocks, dark ribs
        to the left,
    rocks like dinosaur bones,

steps of light,
    each colour the source
        of all the others,
strokes moving the eye,
blocking time's exits,
      blocking light's exits,
        green path winding up,
    strokes leading

to the house (left)
    contend with those moving
        the eye away
    (upper right),
planes of light,
    ridge, scarp,
        resting places
    for different points of view,

strokes moving
    left to right
      at 45°
  juxtaposing

light's exits, time's exits,
        the chorus of strokes
            saying encumbered
    is what we usually are.

L'Estaque, Red Roofs (1883-5)

Pines' repoussoir pushes
    the eye down into
        volumes and planes,
    motley marquetry

of pumpkin orange,
    pepper red, tessellated
        turmeric and saffron
    below a flat wall of sea

and sky. From this far up
    and back, the factory chimney
        is an innocent vertical
    that belongs

as if waiting to frame
    a future seascape,
        not evidence of
    his hated 'invasion

of bipeds' bringing
    'odious' gas-lit quays
        — and — even worse —
    electric light.'

Palette's pursuit
    of changing light,
        certainty
    that shadows must be green

yet whisper and wink
  with lavender, violet,
    rose and blue
  foresaw the future's

analytic eye, ignoring changes
  to the place
    while changing paint:
  the paradox of L'Estaque.

Quotes are from a letter to his goddaughter, Paule Conil, in 1902.

Autumn Landscape (1883-85)

Meissen enamels
are neon in daylight

fumes of colour
rising from stonewashed acids

blasted acrylics
fumes of nothing colours

blanched lavenders
dusty blues inaudible mauves

neon in daylight
stuck at 4 pm all day long

trees are rheumy organs
forgetting to be what they do

someone has pressed his face
close against the scene

clouded it with his breath
and restricted its palette

enamels flare out
tone by tone by tone

in a month we'll see
our breath announcing us

Gardanne (1885-6) / Three paintings

Rue de l'Enfer
  but not Passage du Diable
is just wide enough
  for a handcart

in hill towns perched
  on, scrambling up, spurs
or mounts. Granite rearing
  out of the plain piles

the solid geometry
  of plain walls, ochre
variations, and red
  roofs, clinging on

in a pyramid *brut*,
pushing a church up
into air's heat-heavy
groundmass flashing

and sparking with
  phenocrysts
that are light's constant
liquidations, where form

is facet is form
  in light's constant
liquidations,
  what three paintings show.

At the base somewhere,
  a Chemin des Colombiers
or Charbonniers,
  three pumpkins

on a low wall,
  floats keeping the village
lifted up to the sun,
  lifted up to the sun.

A general poem about still lives

The things of peace,
the works of peace:
apples, onions, lemons,
jug, glass, bottle, plate,
basket, trumpet.
Works and things,
objects for anybody's eye
from anybody's hand.

Works and things
we recognise
as evidence
of everyday operations
but seen as we never can
from multiple perspectives
which imply multiple viewers
so the space in front

of the painting, our ground,
becomes civic, a milieu,
a matrix of views, a commons
where we see not just with him
but are all co-viewers
seeing together the things
of peace, the works of peace,
objects for anybody's eye.

The Politics

I: *Still Life with Apples*
There is no energy
    but where things touch
        energies, sparks
    answering sparks
across the gap
    between lemon
        and tablecloth,
    peach and jug,
the drama of things present
    as themselves
        in the other objects'
  social frame
always fresh.

II: *The Large Bathers*
There are no nymphs or myths
    but flesh as forms
        in air, in light,
    each torso or piled limb
its own dreaming,
    its own standard,
        yet balanced
    by the light's moves
over the soil
    and the three trees
        in a firm base of subtle locks
  that is not yearning
but concord here, now.

Still Life with Cherries and Peaches (1885-87)

— mad scrunched spectacle,
white cloth pushing
boiling cherries, restless,
writhing stalks,
up against the fourth wall
out of vibrating
complementaries,
a shadow world,
partly back-lit,
of glazed green jug
and blue silk drapes
whose gold flecks and flashes
hum quietly in the peaches'
dull orange, dull ochre suede,
vibrating artifice
and nature, the peaches'
lumpy, clod-like peachness
against the cherries'
restless 'what about me?'
highlights, against, in turn,
the painting's underwatery
backstage, the eye chases
the thread or the thread
chases the eye round and round,
the drama never stops
vibrating, outside October gusts,
leaves shatter light,
catch it, juggle it —

Portrait of Jules Peyron (1885-87)

He paints the excise clerk's 'but I'm Montesquiou
at the weekend' wide moustache and pointed beard
dream of dandy. Calm, confident, posing
like this is its forte, the carved face slices
minute after minute, next, next, next,
the carved sockets blankly impatient.

He paints a face that is done with memory,
that has nothing to find: its trigonometry chic
will always work. He paints an origami
of angles, sharp rhythm sequence unscrewing,
tightly untwirling from spiky folds of shirt
and coat to cheek starched for the straight razor.

But then: a final touch hinting at a local joke
between men, at this as a pose of a pose:
touches of weathering and bloom
return the face and the painting and the pose
knowingly, roughly, to its Provençal moment.

*Jules Peyron, excise clerk, witness at Cézanne's wedding,
painted by him twice.*

The Blue Vase (1889-1890)

The painting's noun attire (a vase
of flowers, some fruit, a plate)
dressing its verticals and horizontals
like a thousand others before and after

almost fools us. But then the vase
is all wrong, a bad plasticine model,
unadjusted, out of scale,
made by a kid stuck indoors on a rainy day.

The base is separate from the body
whose shoulders are unequal
and whose scalloped mouth
seems as floppy as a lace collar

forced out of shape to take the blooms
and foliage it's stuffed with,
about to be toppled over
by the bouquet's clumsily flamboyant gesture

it has little right or grace to berth or birth.
They're 'I've had it with flowers' flowers,
damn flowers, bloody flowers, stupid flowers,
ripped up in a great handful

leaves and grass and all and rammed in there,
more cacophony than arrangement.
The vase and the flowers are made
for each other so the vase is stuck

with being as graceless as it is,
looks like it might die with the flowers.
The three apples to the right
keep drawing the eye away

from everything the painting mocks.
'Flowers,' he told Gasquet 'wither
too quickly. I'm giving them up.
Fruits are more reliable.'

Reflections in the Water (c.1890)

Multi-channel
brightness, roughness,
quick strokes fill space,
oil like crayon
shading, combed light
in three levels,
apprehensions:
  sooty scribble,
green emerging,
open yellow.
Roughness, brightness,
  fibrous weaving,
anti-Monet:
  the play of forms
not light, water.
We are sitting
  on the water,
watching space's
self-repeating
kindle, flame out,
ditto, echo;
  echo, ditto.

Woman with Coffee Pot (1890-4)

A metal postcard
where she is a machine,

bodice's carapace, blue steel
scored and cut like shutters,

gilled sheet bent and hammered
at the same bench as the mug,

the giant spoon, the coffee pot.
Resting hands

of clumsy painted wood,
blocky, mannish head

and Gioconda self-regard
add unconvincing touches

of 'humanity', 'reality'.
Panels on the wall behind

could be the artist's works,
say there's nothing outside

the frame, outside the paint,
beyond this metal postcard.

Tulips in a Vase (1892)
for Johanna Malt

Three red tulips,
    stems and leaves turning dark,
dark angelica, muddied chartreuse,
       growing heavy with coming rot,
    flowers unwrapping
       the torn paper of their tulipness,
          leaving it behind,
    slumping comfortably
into half-lives
    of failed definition,
       poor description.

The dark green vase,
    misshapen like a reject,
adds to a stubborn sense
       of meaninglessness embraced,
    the painting shaking us awake
      from the paint,
          from florists' and academicians' dreams
    of perfect flowers,
to see what caught his eye,
    the base's blushing flesh
       of green, yellow, red, mauve.

Note: This poem is 'for Johanna Malt' because it was written shortly after hearing her keynote address at the Hull ekphrasis conference and reading her article 'Leaving traces: surface contact in Ponge, Penone and Alÿs' (Word & Image, 29.1: 92-104.)

The House with Cracked Walls (1892-4)

House giving itself back
  to the trees and the rocks
(as common as the towns
  piled on hills like croquembouche)
house granite's abandoned
variation on itself

House giving itself back
  to the trees and the rocks
the harsh laughter of the heat
  that cooks what's built to biscuit
expands metals swells
  beer merchants' wallets

House giving itself back
  to the trees and the rocks
your cracks echoed by and echo
  the shape of the trees
your cracks and the trees
  riff on affinities

House giving itself back
  to the trees and the rocks
image of how easily care
slips from our grasp
of how hard it is to position
ourselves on this earth

House giving itself back
  to the trees and the rocks
syntax once for someone's time here
now not a story anymore

there is no word for a broken pot
  or a broken house

Note: Lines 5 and 6 in stanza two draw on Cézanne's
letter to his son, 8 September 1906.

Curves, Bends

The road bends
into the countryside

and the eye,
leaning into

each curve,
finds its desire

lured deeper,
drawn farther into,

the unseen minutes
that bend, unbend,

become, become.
The eye leans

into the countryside
and the road,

drawing together
wall and tree,

house and hill,
place and trace,

before it darts
behind outcrop

or gets lost
in a thicket.

Still Life with Ginger Jar
and Eggplants (1893)

The table is set,
    for different orders
        or oddments
of orders, to be
in mute contact
    but writing one over
        another
over the one.

White cloth, torn metal
    explosion flower,
        horrid beak curve,
at its point, a plate
of fruit, impossibly
    served, against blue cloth
        patterned with leaves
and flowers,

mimicking here
    amphora, ur-jar,
        there a burst bag
of spilling guts.
The rounded ginger jar,
    raffia-corded, picks up
        the blue cloth's blue,
washes it out,

then moves the eye
    from its open mouth
        to the open mouth
of the large green jar

which, in its turn,
    moves the eye to
        to the watermelon's sphere
    in looping questions

about kinds or strains
    or family trees
        in form's gene pool.
    The three eggplants,
black fruit dangling
    off a stripped, forked pole,
        one to the fore,
    may be rude fun

about trees or progeny,
    find it or miss it,
        its energy muted
    in the painting's larger loop
of different orders
    or oddments of orders
        writing one over
    another over the one.

Still Life with Plaster Cupid (1894)

The painting shifts
on the putto's hips
that twist the floor
until it lifts
and tilts and tips
and a giant apple
does not roll but rolls
the eye and the eye's
'why not?' back down
to the table's plot
where the putto strides
through fruit and veg
and an outsize onion
is on the table
and in the world
of the still life leant
against the wall,
the still life
whose blue cloth spills
out of the frame
to where the putto stands
and twists and shifts
the painted space
around his hips.

The Card Players (1892-5, 1894-5)

I – (1892-5)

Slowed to two frames
    a second, a present
        moment where a wonky,
    red-clay table glows
with more life than two men,
    volumes as much as figures,
        old pinhead with giant's knees
    vs. more proportioned younger man,
growing old in the playing out
    of unbroken custom,
        slowed to two frames
    a second, a present
moment deepens, lengthens,
    yawns, yawns and dust falls,
        settles almost audibly,
    staining colours with time,
ochres, browns, rough graphics,
    as two men play beyond
        desire or chance.

II – (1894-5)

Slowed to two frames
    a second, a present
        moment where a wonky,
    red-clay table glows,
burns and pulses,
    acts in the same nervy drama
        of the next card
    as two men who seem lit
from within, enlightened
    in an endlessly lengthening,
        deepening minute,
    around which the world
stops spinning, a minute
    where they arrange everything,
        the light on each other's jackets,
    the pulse in each other's flesh,
the bright abstract pastoral
    that opens behind them,
        then make their play.

Millstone and Cistern in the Undergrowth (1892-94)

The woods rethought,
structure of strokes,
plates and facets
reassembled,

scaffolding
coloured in with
green's take on
desert colours,

burnt earth beneath.
    The title rings
first Valéry's
'sonore citerne'

(booming cistern,
echoey tank),
then his poem's
setting 'Midi

juste' (impartial
noon), same Midi
that, each second,
    burns more, burns more

into the air
    at Chateau Noir.
Echoey woods,
just air and noon,

impartial earth
  the burnt millstone
burns back into.
  Rethought colours,

reassembled titles,
structure of seconds,
Midi's facets,
  desert and green

ring each other's
  sonorities.
The cistern booms
  beneath the trees.

Winter Landscape, Giverny (1894)

Air's hinges creak

in the stiff light.

Bare orchard barely

itself, trees wispy

as smoke, dirty ribbons

in the grey breeze.

The orchard wall,

the gable end,

wobble and give up,

colour as struggle and loss.

Raw canvas mist

clearing, hanging.

Lac d'Annecy (1896)

En vacance en famille | 'It's temperate here' | he wrote Gasquet
| 'And nature a little like | we've been taught| by young ladies'
albums' | so he painted the lake | as everything | he and it |
were not

the tree's brooding fringe, | mountains as split | and shattered
slate, | reflections in the lake | turning it to scored crystal |
glass crudely etched | or reflections themselves | turned to blue
chalk cliffs

first sun striking | the tree | the chateau | is smashed by the
tree's tangle | into a sky | and one lit hillside of | mauve | pink
| green | yellow | blue | scales | splinters | shards | diamonds
| all sections moving all the time

it's as if | he catches first sun surprising | the world in dark
dreams | of obduracy | of unloveliness

it's as if | he embraces certainty of structure | only to tip it |
crack it | mock it | shatter it

it's as if | he catches first sun surprising | the world in dark
dreams of being | a hard thing | a machine made of rocks |
roots | water |

In the Woods - 3 (1898)
(Undergowth)

Something is running
    through the blue woods,
        so blue, all blue,
    running away
from each stroke and dab
    catching at, chasing
        from left to right,
    right to left.

Light is running,
    time is running,
        through the blue woods —
    just when light's settled,
you move, and it moves,
    jumping from leaf
        to leaf,
    jerking the brush

from thing to form.
    Raw canvas is light
        breaking through
    or the brush firing
and missing or the blue woods,
    all blue, so blue,
        laughing, laughing,
    'your eye is nothing'

meaning 'your eye has it
    but your hand's too slow'

Still Life with (Red) Onions and Bottle (1898)

Each stroke flies into the singular,
like disconnects, free accents on
the top of the cork and an
onion's base.
        The wineglass
stem, off-centre, too far right,
keys a drama of poles
and pivots, turning points;
the onion,
        central in its lack
of centre, unlike the apple,
less solid somehow in its layers
and skins and micro-layers,
in its known but unseen
translucence.
        To be grounded
like an apple, each onion
would have to spin in space.
The wineglass stem
a variant
        of onion shoots
and vice versa, elements
of a proposition reversed
as if each refracts each
and form needs form
needs form.
        And the bottle (left)
and the cloth billowing
off the table? The blown glass
says all is design, the cloth
all is feeling; the desire
for the sign, the sign
escaping, escaping.

Millstone in the Park at Château Noir
(1898-1900)

…turning the page quickly back
forth back forth back forth *Bathers,*
The Large Bathers, Millstone blur,
overlaid transparencies,
bodies rocks bodies rocks rocks,
the same sprawled forms, oblong blocks
stretched out like legs or sunning
backs, I see a belly's curve
meet haunch, groin and shadowed crotch
in piled up abandoned stone
that seems to be returning
to the earth or getting just
this far out of it, turning

the page quickly back forth back,
I think the bathers' bodies
are slathered with drying mud,
forms in their own first light, old
as the earth and very new,
as if bare flesh is always
for a moment hopeful as
cut stone in the cutting blinks
at the future, bodies rocks,
oblong, rectangular blocks,
the trees can barely stand up,
stand as if they've been flattened,
with a piney twang sprung back…

Bathers and More Bathers

'For in truth nature is our first language. Our bodies remember!'
Jacques Lecoq, *Le Corps Poétique*

In the age of the engineer | take the body out of the studio | in
the republic of straight lines | take it outside | naked flesh | the
play of light on it | joins the language | of water | grass | trees |
sky | light on water | shadow on leaf

naked flesh | the play of light on it | allows the body | the same
geometry | as everything else | limbs | torsos | standing or
sprawled | the interplay | of crooked arms | bent knees | curved
backs | are forms | answering to | forms

these bodies | at rest | could fuck | or wrestle | but wear desire |
like they wear light and shade | these bodies at rest | are ancient
ease | or ideal future | naked flesh | the play of light on it |
another way | of getting nature | to reveal itself

Note: The phrase about engineers and straight lines are taken from
Cézanne *by Joachim Gasquet.*

The Bottle

In the beginning
   was the bottle

      you find everywhere,
  just getting on with it,

glugging out *le jaja*
   lunchtimes,

      on the big table
  in the village bar.

Another part
   of the work;

      like the faucille
or the hammer,

another piece
   of the commune's net

      of tools and trade.
  Its red/green,

green/black, black/red,
   green/blond

      knows the darkness
  of a neighbour's cave,

the unswept shadows
   under a bench,

          the absurd, desperate lodging
      of a deep coat pocket.

The bottle.
     Here it is:

         found among apples
    or onions

or on a shelf
     like an icon.

         The subject
    of every verb.

The simple bottle.
     Waiting to be grasped.

Le jaja: wine for everyday.
faucille: sickle.
cave: cellar.

Trees by the Water (1900)
watercolour on paper

Colour's brief visit
    to the paper

graphs the body's
    mime of fluxes

on its axes,
    in its forces,

so the trees are axes
    for clusters, patches,

that mime fluxes
    in colours' feelings,

feelings' colours,
    as spectres colour

barely catches,
    hardly coaxes,

to the paper,
    where a shelf

of mist suggests
    morning.

Pyramid of Skulls (1901)

D'ailleurs en ce temps léthargique
Sans gaîté comme sans remords,
Le seul rire encore logique,
C'est celui des têtes de morts
                    Paul Verlaine, 'Quatrain'

Fruit on a table hums with songs
we know well. Piled skulls, pressed up
against the window of the painting,
jawless, in your face, tease us to reach

for distorting profundities. The painting
takes the shape of our days, which we
heartily police to be round or square
or whatever suits the spouting

of our heart's own policies, and pulls
and twists and scrunches their beloved
soft geometry until an edge buckles
and breaks and we are faced with skulls

looping and looping back to themselves
and each other, perpetual echoes
of a glyph. The two lower ones seem reduced,
smoothed, baked and earthy, primitive vessels

to be blown or drunk from, as if an interest
in round volumes with holes had got the better of the
brush. The top one is white, stonier, harsher,
newer perhaps, shouting today's news

about skulls which is that here on the table
is piled a curious kind of debris or rubbish
and, stranger perhaps, a thought of drought
always comes to mind from the way

the sockets are yearning. And this is one way
that skulls, piled on a table in a pyramid,
pressed up against the window of the painting
might make something happen in us.

Woman in Blue (c. 1902)

The perfect understanding
    between the still life
        and the portrait.
    In the fractional

seconds of the brush,
    an apple, a bottle,
        lose thingness,
    become presences,

movements of energy,
    through gestures, poses,
        the everyday eye
    never notices, misses.

Under the same brush,
    figures grow stiff,
        immobile, lose presence
    and gain thingness,

like this woman,
    carved crystal armour,
        cool blue stone,
    negatively charged,

the hat a maquette
    in plaster or dark glass.
        The scored lines,
    the incisions

in the sulphite details
    of shoulder flounces
        like tiered roofs,
    of stiff lapels

and elbow creases,
    accent joints,
        evoke not inner life
    but armature.

The face, downcast,
    distant, empty,
        unknowable,
    completes the picture

of a notness paused in,
    powered down from
        waiting for
    its whatness.

Still Life with Ginger Jar,
Sugar Bowl and Oranges (1902-06)

Tectonic uplift
    of a landscape
        with things in it,
    cloth heavy
with candied leaves,
    with dried-on splashes
        of apricot or pumpkin
    toned flowers
interpreting the orange
    of the fruit floating
        on its buckled rhombus
    crumple zones.

Ginger, oranges,
    sugar less so,
        exotic once
    now muted
as the landscape
    where the straw-webbed jar,
        lidded bowl and flattened dish
    grow louder
in their blue-white, white-blue
    whiteness and switch on
        the fulgent flavedo
    of the fruit

and the eye, re-trained,
    sees the landscape
        fluoresce.

Postcard from Aix

Painting
is a way
of not knowing
everything
the city tells us
is waxed and shining
because knowing
is a way
of not looking
at what the city
names for us
so what painting
finds out it thinks
and looks to name
is opposite
somehow
to the waxed and shining,
already named,
since, being painted,
it is never
the thing, only
its moments
of being heard
in the eye,
felt on the mind,
always turning
that way and this
inside what names
the paint bestows
yet somehow
always squared
with the certainty of its place
in history,
geometry.

Rocks Near the Caves
above the Chateau Noir (1904)

The eye's motor motors,
activates the figures
of when and what
seeding then boiling
each other into steam
that, condensing, falls
as the poverty
or thickness
of the next moment
that bobs somewhere
always ahead of the hand
and the brush
that together rewrite
the history of their moves
in the physique of sight
as a new history
of the eye's motor
activating the forms
of fleeting solids
and heavy light
as tectonic plates
of colour that remember
how once boulders boiled
though now their what
is the trees' when.

The Big Trees (1904)

Creak whirr whistle
    scrape go the trees
        of the mechanical wood
  as you're drawn in

under the twisted
    rusty iron racks
        of the big trees
  by a thin central pole,

the big trees scalded
    and bent into hooks
        and prongs in pressure
  waves of Provençal heat,

under a canopy
    of blue glass
        as the paint slows down
  to catch wavelengths

hitting leaves,
    as you're drawn in
        under a canopy
  of raw canvas

clerestories
    picking out patchworks
        of autumn tones,
  chlorophyll degrading.

The Gardener Vallier (1906)

— resequenced swatches,
dazzled blues and flesh tones,
discover movement
and lines of force
on a relaxed body
in a shady corner,
a body that is everything
the painting body cannot be,
oil soft and weightless
as watercolour, as quick
as pastel, floats the soft hat,
the baggy shirt, the crossed legs
still vibrating,
youthfully flung a minute past,
as events of light
that might, the next minute,
discover nothing,
and so the figure emerges
from dark dabs that could be
ivy overhanging —

The White

White holes
    in the late works,
        wounds in colour,
   cuts in light,

between fruits and
    tablecloth,
        or on the mountain,
   keep opening.

White hungers,
    keeps colours restless,
        gap and tone,
   trend and edge

trembling against
    each other, never sleep,
        fizzing spectacle
   of lived space.

White opens
    centres of gravity
        for desires
   that cannot aver,

holes in precision
    that are precision,
        dissonances
   that form planes'

placeless places.
    White opens.
        Silence gives form
   to music.

The Rage

Mont Sainte-Victoire's
    turdy pile.
        The cut-off tent pole
    triangle of trees

in *Les Grandes Baigneuses*.
    More trees, black,
        dried-blood red,
    bluer than the sky

and hammering on it
    like a drum
        in *Le Cabanon*
    de Jourdan.

The brush draws
    the eye upwards,
        its strokes sobbing
    and splitting the air

with a passionate,
    despairing cry
        that the rocks, trees,
    roads and houses

we lump into sentences
    for our crude drama
        must be understood
    by their opposite

— the limitless sky,
    the uncontainable light.
        This is the end of rage,
    thirty years

of nothing else,
　　in the face of light's
　　　　changing expressions,
　　making contours

impossible.
　　The sky thrums and twangs
　　　　with the aftershocks
　　of what it swells

and arches over:
　　all the time,
　　　　the world increasing
　　terribly.

Gestures of the Eye

old stones
in old mortar
distinct steps
with steps missing
unquiet packages
of light from blue
to tan no flow
tugging the eye
restlessly rearranging
with each shuttering
and throwing open
sometimes cream is grey
butter wet sand
or green becomes orange
the self constantly
blending harmonising
chasing the imp
of linearity
or how could we live
with so much unbled
so much clanging
above the motley walls
a steady gaze
burns
a notional blue
from a clear sky
leaving it unpainted
the summit
a white square
full of rubbish
washing over
the eyeballs
cataclysms
of motes and fibres
x-rays writhing luminous

full of swallows
clipping insects
out of the air
or drifting
on their blades

Cézanne at Mont Sainte Victoire

Cézanne painted Mont Sainte Victoire
more than 60 times between 1870 and 1906

Shingles of colour
    clattering
        over the mountain
    are the mountain,
jolts firing oc
    randomly
        oc oc,
    in Provençal air,
hot, cold, hot,
    like raw blocks

        in the silty nougat
    of gable ends
where colour's
    what jarred the spade
        or set the scythe on edge
    in worked earth,
a harmony
    of whims.
        The moment
    of this rock's not stuck

in the moment of that rock
    or this tree,
        but as deeply felt
    as any love or parting
then analysed.
    The paint
        is neither repair
    nor regret:

the brush stops
    first this then that

        tinkling mirror
    and finds, sometimes,
that tone and colour
    are haunted gaps,
        the anguish
of a necessary lack.

The brush clatters
    and tumbles
        over the mountain,
    white opening shocks,

dabs then blocks,
    in the late works,
        fallings short of light's
    never-ending 'what
has happened here',
    as the landscape
        thinks him deeper
    into its violent body.
The colours move
    further apart,

        do not come back.
    All mountains are terrible.